THE COUNTING HOUSE

The Counting House

Sandra Ridley

BookThug

2013

The production of this book was made possible through the generous assistance of the Canada Council for the Arts and the Ontario Arts Council.

 Canada Council **Conseil des Arts**
for the Arts **du Canada**

 ONTARIO ARTS COUNCIL
CONSEIL DES ARTS DE L'ONTARIO
50 YEARS OF ONTARIO GOVERNMENT SUPPORT OF THE ARTS
50 ANS DE SOUTIEN DU GOUVERNEMENT DE L'ONTARIO AUX ARTS

LIBRARY AND ARCHIVES CANADA CATALOGUING IN PUBLICATION

Ridley, Sandra, 1973-, author
      The counting house / Sandra Ridley.

Poems.
Issued in print and electronic formats.
ISBN 978-1-927040-84-3 (PBK.). – ISBN 978-1-927040-94-2 (EPUB). –
ISBN 978-1-77166-026-6 (MOBI). – ISBN 978-1-77166-027-3 (PDF).

      I. Title.

PS8635.I344C69 2013   C811.6   C2013-905138-4
                                          C2013-905139-2

Printed in Canada

Table of Contents

A General Tale

A husha.

A husha.

According to and fittingly — a break
and our pockets fill with flowers to conceal the smell of dying.

Thus concludes the final succumbing to bloody pomander and posy.

The only authentic reference being a ring — a ring of roses
moreover and other than this
covenant
for happiness.

Eventually.

We would have — O, we would have.

Falling — not always a dropping to the ground
construed
as rhyme not death
not a literal fall or heartbreak
instead (but)
any other form of respective bending.

Though all evidence points strongly
against — a worn rose — (once) (once) (once) popular conjecture.

Now complex gossip.

(Continue to writhe.)

If this is like nothing else
find a different interpretation over time.

I deny I fell — I curtsied
for a rogue disinterest
then left.

(No evidence.)

Unfurled — each underhanded
anonymous
note.

Twenty-four blackbirds for twenty-four hours.

A maiden bandied — a malediction.

Passing fancy.

Who once loved to watch you sleep?

Betray a true portrayal — scantily for palatability.

A dainty banter.

You're happiest after.

THE END is a wretched death.

O, fool or esoteric fabulist who sacrificed a parlour archetype.
If you don't have what you want —
recant.

                                        Recount a little wiser.

O, shrouded king who caught this blood, a ruby thimble full
of mourning.

You once watched me from afar without knowing who I was.

Shove a high bird into a pie — then cut out your regal ending
with irreverence for the heart alive.

      (O, be alive-o.)

          Pay sixpence for a honeyed woe. (Be spoon-fed and revived.)

          As a queen languishes in her reliquary — as a lady hangs
          a line of feathered robes.

              Say then, this can be lasting, may be calm. Say, still.
              Say, O, I do.

              And, really, I (still) do.

                              Say, Love, O, how does your garden?

You were my Sanctus.

I was your ringing glory.

I held a pretty cockleshell because I was not pretty.

I was your shrine.

Lone in the garden — lamented.

Your opinion was different.

Your theory on how roses should grow.

O, how you worked on your Eden for twenty-four years.

Restate my (re)cited biblical source.

I am reasonably ashamed. (O, whore hellion!)

Your devil.

A silver bell rang out —

foreshadowing

a signal

someone shall cry

(O, how she cried)

and

twenty-four birds shall arrive

and

four and twenty die —

each dwindling a ribbon

with a silver bell.

Carry the coffin.

Love.

Carry the link.
Dig the grave. All night.

(A-sighing and a-sobbing.)

I said —

I.

I.

I.

Lax Tabulation

Recent/irreconcilable

in closure (of course)   in fact   there is no evidence   suspect

this lapse   a coincidence   my strange disappearance   unaccounted

delivered by *cortège*   each time I leave   shall be my last

Recent/questionable

another regression   abandoned   a little more slowly   unsurely

accompanied by   faint sounds   (my vulgar grace)   how can I smile   like that

knowing what I've done

Recent/discernible

patient   and pinioned   for the composition of   a footnote

for nothing   when there is no peril   Love   I tried to abide your theme

Recent/pieced-together

a manifest disorder	in the course of time	a predisposition	a poem ignorant of failing
a motif executed	(a sin)	in the end	(cunning faith)

Recent/failed

(*Ibid.*)

Recent/overwhelming miserable miserable

a proposition	tell-taled	don't write love	with Wilkins' letterpress
pettifog	a feeble mockery	of another	splendoured literature

Recent/last

a presaged   claret burden   in a sequence of dates   the most recent

disturbing reversal   you covet your dandy fancy   when I once was

depicted as muse-ic   your ink dissolves   all excess

Recent/précis

au current   a cowled silhouette   you see me   impure

but I am most impure   which you valued (candid)   so what if I can't stay   Love

you never expected I would

Recent/apparent

you already doubt   this haunting   vanity   prefigured

by insinuating the sullen   in counting follies   (contrary)   and weak-kneed

lie in want

Recent/perpetual

by necessity   a fool   but you are most foolish   love

ranked highest   among your vices   (possessing)   the lauded

as your absolved   absolute

Recent/fraught

nothing different   another pleasured gesture   gentled

in failure   embodied in the prone position

as feebleness   manifesting vulgar   (indulgence forfeited)

and glossed falsely

Recent/subversive

left to yourself   in feigned resolution   from the last lurid criticism   a besotted denouement

but   in fact   a simple sudden shunning

Recent/bewildered

two witnesses ·   and their authority   inviolate

guardians and protectors   alluded   I won't tell you

there were two witnesses   this is assuredly encouraging

Recent/ferocious

hereto   appertaining to   each act of force   deemed necessary

notwithstanding   and notwithstanding   each new confinement

Recent/vexed

abandoned   the other half   surreptitiously   under ethic and obligation

certainly   lascivious

and given up   to others   (with all others)   disgraced

Recent/unfinished

if lately   my leaving was expected   unequivocal and necessary

if for reasons   a fractious double role   your (pilloried) dialectic failed to provoke

Recent/chronicled

ruined fervour   a variation on a theme   tirelessly repeated   in every literary model

before virtue   vilified   you condemn   my common faults

Recent/apparent

that is   I am truthful   (the most common of my faults)

to censure criticism   that is   an atrocious deception

as a footnote error   a merciful absence   unforeseen

as judgment   a just punishment

Recent/less fictive

each act   a revision   in the strictest sense   a lie

decrying   there are two readers   discordant   in accruing lines

Recent/self-evident

a sequence of dates   thereto (appertaining to)   margins

and footnotes of   the salacious   proper to

and nonetheless   the weak   entrusted isolated categories

Recent/denounced

rage in narrowed limits   at the most extreme point   attenuated

Recent/undressed (respectable)

the strength of immediacy	Love	you need to protect yourself
on certain days	you say	you are afraid
I scare you	no	you scare yourself

Recent/palatable

once read	on occasion	it's been violent	insofar as
in spite of	and without consequence	being too disjunct	too applicable
a priori	petits fours of truth		

Recent/hand held vicious

digressed	and given	a lack of reference	and without recourse to
the rigorousness of	discipline	and without recourse to	a disturbance
hastening insistence	brutalized		

Recent/gainsaid

the very requirement of confinement   (no refuge for joy)   suffering

reckoned   in private form

Recent/discretion

maudlin   bellicose   but not complaisant   (painstaken)

and banished inclinations turn   the page   as another line consoles

Recent/belles-lettres

words   set apart   whether or not

you admit   this distinction

not concerning that   but   concerning   a transgression

apparently   only   two readers recount   what you've done

Recent/explicit

a perceptible gesture	multiple and accumulated	prolonged	and gradually
more remote		kisses	felt like kisses
(behaviour)	forthwith	and	denied

Recent/subsequent

such	suddenly	intensified	frenzied then degenerated
an aberrant idea	disassociated	and comprised of	surrendering
henceforth separated	and unkempt	(unkempt)	I can't feel a difference

Recent/unashamed

sullied	this lack		extenuated
a pure spectacle	relentlessly	(lax)	each calumny insults

Recent/ghosted

hopeless   most hopeless   I left

                                                                                 my life

Recent/equivocal

revision as sacrifice   as revelation   dismayed

and debased   as disappearance   the fret of each line

Recent/detailed various

a vagary   or at least an explanation   signifying a change

deviating   an avowal   of my own accord

to disclose   (this sang-froid)   dignified

Recent/visible

you have already read so   (uttered)   you consorted   indiscriminately

and glorified   unguised   (and still)   flaunt this everywhere

Recent/benediction

this grief   antipathy   assuredly acknowledged   but given no pretext

confessed   a *bête noire*   a locket   your casket latch

Testamonium

I.

Unafraid. She takes her own hair by the fistful. Your Darling. Undoubtedly. Deserving or not. Offers penitence with a punishment.

This is unacceptable.

Each privation forbidden to her. By her. Gradually. Affections will become more harmful.

Vengeful.

Seething.

She confuses murmurs with furies.

Shuns night-company.

Stupefied.

You are not capable of being moved.

II.

Apologist.

                                        You seem different.

You want a more decent measured speech. Meeker language.

          Your Darling concedes she has always been present. From the beginning.
          Her entrance was neither deceptive. Nor delicately feigned.

III.

Unabraded.

    Bitten hands.

    Your Darling explains the excessive. The manic.

    Calm as constraint.

    Each agitation won't cease to affect her. Bitten hands. Bitten lip. The eventual provoked. Convinces you. The inappropriate (of course) reciprocal.

                Your Darling repeats.

Hysteric. Sickeningly. Always unwilling to please.

    In such a state. She is not.

    Your sonorous body. Your nervous type.

    Offer a sympathy. An indelicate subtlety. It's certain that she can't explain her association. In relation to. At the same time. Her confinement.

    Responsive to your state of vigilance.

            Who celebrates a shrivelling?

Turn your back upon the tightening deductive. How perceptive your closest contradictions.

Uncertainly citing against her absence of extravagance.

      Poise.   Charm.

IV.

Your Darling reveals her strength in proportion to her weakness. Pell-mell. Discriminately personal. Vainly sumptuous.

> She returns with uncontrolled moments of joy. Unmeasured.
> Forgets how quickly and assuredly she once withdrew.

Unvanquished.

A ruse is a ruse and ceaselessly. She gave up. Abandoned heart and vitriol.

Your Darling is vulgar in all of her violet forms.

V.

An aspect of repetition.

Each subsequent act derived from the gentleness of brief pleasure.

        Beholden. She meant to. (Didn't mean to without discipline.)

Your Darling insufficiently restricted. Hesitates in proportion. The way you would have her. Diminished. Precisely lacking. Her taint spreads at threatening speed.

In fact. This is constant. Complicit with failure. When your Darling is surrounded by others. By all others. She hears the detailed various. *She said. She did.*

        In more recent times. Less legitimately constrained.

        Remorse.

        In reckoning the intricacies. Your Darling will choose an example. (Taken.)

        A burdensome note. Another example given from elsewhere.
        There will be no confusion about the admittance.

Her resistance was not exceptional.

Her *supplice*. After losing restraint.

                                  Exquisite pain.

VI.

Upheaval from the onslaught. Before. Foolishness as consolation.
A handwritten missive as promissory.

Envoi unsent.

Reticence.

Peculiar to her.

Less reasoned discourse. A barbarous intimate remittance.

A proposal you take frightful. Nothing more then than this. Incessant.
Interrogation. A prolonged succession of questions.

Aversion. Without vindication.

A frivolity. Your Darling leaves you untouched.

VII.

Although there is continuity. There has always been. What does this account for?
The time of the spectacle. One difficulty. Then the following.

                                                                    You were sullied.

Solemnly.

Feel nothing.

There is certainly something wrong.

Preclude the incredulous. In order to control. A wreck. A wretch. It seems. She must be such.
In theory. Or rather. In dream. As early as. Before long. Appearing indecipherable. A villain.

Such.

A delinquent.

                                                                    Irreverent.

                                                                    What she has done.

Your Darling. All bound up.

VIII.

Dissipate the cherished at an astonishing rate. Apropos of the villain.

You are born out of nought.
No background. No origin. In a double sense.

No story.

(Duplicitous.)

Take back with your hands what you gave with your mouth.

Rescind the intolerable.

Then make distant.

Consider your Darling docile. Efface her.

Sorry.

Compulsory and accumulated.

Revelled less sincere.

IX.

A slight torment. You are not inclined to share. Perhaps. In any case. It is unimportant. Maligned with discretion. Without deviation. Taciturn. Your reiterated silence.

(Of course.) It happened.

                                                    But.

                                                    It was very late.

You were compelled.

X.

A gentler lesson then. *Deserved.* Repeated as often as possible. Propose her more reasonable. Present her with a pleasant disposition. For most general acceptance.

                                                        A lasting positive impression.

Next time.

Give in to a blithe variety of vice.

Be more vigilant. Refute. Rectify through penance. In a strictest sense. Above all. Be forthright. Reject and disdain. The trifle of your indulgence.

Your ledger. The value of evidence. Descried. No longer as you once were.

Miserable.

As if you were right.

                                                                    She was illicit.

         (Only partly.)

                                    Display a form of sadness.

XI.

Chamber walls. Ghosted letters. *I abhor you.*

A villain. A victim. Unmotivated by love. Or fear. Or the prospect of. Therefore. Hitherto. Recognized. Thereby. Brought to bear.

> Your Darling will learn to be more prudent.

Carry associated moments. Divisible into as many portions as paucities. With neither the desire. To repeat. Nor the possibility. In particular. Carry a requisite consequence.

Unmitigated and notoriously illustrious. At this moment. A quarrel.

Abrupt.

XII.

Never call her by her name. Your Darling. Clandestine.

Such is not possible. Unless (of course). Such is possible.

Continue to writhe. For there has always been curiosity. Strict inquisitions.
You are insidious. *Where have you been? With whom?*

Your permitted versus that unbidden.

Unexplained.

As if the encounter took place without you. (Denial of the witness.)
The absolute privilege of unknowing. Impossible.

There is no identity of even you.

Accuser.

XIII.

Rely on the scarcity of your senses. Each requires the other.
Find your Darling.

                               Unfulfilled.

                               If not exactly. Directly. At very least. Of the opinion.
                               Your Darling came home late.

                               Caught up.

                               Not in a position to answer.

                                                   Unready.
                                     Instructed. Entrusted.

                                     Presented.
                                     Examined.

                                 Found sufficiently slight.

                                     Conformed.
                                     Presented.

                                     Ready.

                                   Indisposed.
                                   Undergone.

                                   Complaisant.

Lay her down according to discipline.

XIV.

Assume this is based on this. Fact perhaps. Truthfully even. A response to the unembellished. (Recent.) This is why. That is why. This is unlamentable.

Difficult. More restrictive.

Roughly speaking.

Lecherous.

Your proclivity will break her down.

Brocade her.

Indulge in tenderness.
It is false.

An ordeal.

The most treacherous form.

Such is the effect of reassurance.

Bestow a wilted bouquet.

XV.

You began with love. Unfailing. Intended invariably. Love always involves a degree of pain.
In that. Constancy.

The possessor never explicitly admitted or denied. Nor alleviated.

The discreet lasts only a moment. Comes vengeful.

> The morning before.

> The decline.

> The spectacle.

Your hold on her body will not entirely disappear.

XVI.

A privilege. She was not so much. Or not only. Or not in any way fundamental. She was rather. In service to your excess. Especially. Or rather. For the most part.

She was alone.

XVII.

When your Darling considers it. If she was concerned with it then. Aware of the sundries. Details. Despair became a whole history.

She had a lack of willingness. Insufferable. Her crudest form.

With the same persistence. She cedes to tendency. Falls with a rigorous ferocity.

Perpetually.

        Bitten hands.

                Bitten lip.

Each imposition accrued a certain benefit. A response. A catechism given willingly. Or by force. A little later. Verified. You relegated her to a bed where you attached your true name.

                                  There.

Your Darling remains.

Her body more constant than her mind.

                Beside herself.

                          Be reassured.

At this moment. Her little death is a type of succession.
In this sense. She succeeds.

XVIII.

Befitting your point of view.

Not inclined to risk positing. Specifically.

For nothing of consequence as she was never there.

> On the appointed day. Your Darling shall leave. Were you to let her fix a date. (Of course.) She should not choose. Nor would you have her.

Suitably. It will be a glorious day. What a pity the last went unremarked.

Such is the mark of the blessed.

XIX.

Each ambiguity explicitly unpalatable. Each punitive.
Proof.

Within each.
A comparable violence.

The truth is wretched. That is. The inseparable truth.

                                        Your Darling is most wretched.

Discourage her.

XX.

This then your countenance. The essential. Hastened. Clearer.

A fable more fearsome. Full of vengeance.

                  Your cruelty. A lesson for her.

                            Her raiment of disobedience.

                            Deportment. Her mere glance and gesture.

Par excellence. Your Darling responds. Persuasive. (Inexorable.)
Detached.

She shall leave.

Abandon every letter.

XXI.

Gradually. In prolonged succession. With the same insistence. Passing days of pain.

XXII.

Refuse your Darling her comforts.

The ordeal.

The ordeal again.

Not as you might imagine it.

Greater.

Or rendered lesser.

Bearable.

The body's habit of revoking. That is to say. She is undisciplined through each reciprocal gesture. Aside from your intentions. Nonetheless. Lastly. Her objection.

Mediocre through a series of minor distinctions.

There will be no end to the ridicule.

Assigned to her place. She shall leave it.

She said. She did.

Expressly forbidden.

Your Darling detaches.

Her role.

XXIII.

Immodest perversities accepted easily when you have no influence or control. Each malingering. Forthright. Not a matter of indifference.

Indiscreet. Inspection as ritual.

Suspicion.

XXIV.

The push of your hands is useless. Insidious. Deceitful. Her being without being seen. Constantly. Under your gaze.

>
> Her down.
>
> Quiet.
>
> Smothering.
>
> You are not comporting properly. Strong hold of the body. She is flawed. (Quite flawed.) No and no. Specifically. You are rigorous.

Don't.

Begin.

Your Darling displayed.

Look who can.

She is neither heartened. Nor consoled.

Most vigilant. Or not sleeping.

Unmoved by any outward sign.

XXV.

After losing constraint. An absence. She became a sort. Furthermore. Furthermore.
In ravishing fashion.

Banished.

You were inspired by your malice. In that moment. You felt such pleasure.

Until recently.

                                                                She was not a threat.

XXVI.

Harm exhausted.

This is not the first time. The body in the grip. Apparently. A gesture.
Another consequent account.

Brazen. Bitten lip. Bite marks on the hands.

Habitual acts of sacrilege.

Simply.

(Slowly.)

Unexulted. Undocile.

Trembling on the verge.

A wretch.

She beseeched a particular care.

XXVII.

Given brevity. Intention versus result. Or repetition. The very act of tabulation. The bitter tally. *You said. She did.* Your Darling of her own volition.

Slap-dashed versus reward.

She shall decide how long this will last and conclude.

Her own accord.

XXVIII.

No doubt. Each redress will spurn you.

                                                                    Affronted.

Portrayed. Out of proportion.

                                              Bruiser.

No doubt. Her incorrect tone becomes baleful. An example given to others. She dares.
An indirect reply. Sudden cunning. Slackened. Shameful. (Of course.)

Your opinion.

Your conviction.

She shall not cease.

                                                        (*Your* most horrible cry.)

Word for word. Her salutary objection.

She lives.

She lives wicked.

XXIX.

Barbaric. With rigour. With ferocity. Benevolence attenuated.

Dreadful. This decline.

Vulgar.

Your ruin. Corrective. Meticulous. She shall not forget. Once. Not only. Not only. But also. (Not only.) The coercion of the body. Closing. When once such wetness.

Your aversion. Your most vicious affinities. Contrary. Under duress. Scarcely credible. Ceasing amends.

You should not have been surprised.

No trace of you on her.

No smell. (Of course.) You of no name.

Bitten hands.

Bitten lip.

She will lie. You say.

Declare weakly.

Your Darling undressed will press back against the cold floor.

XXX.

The art of rectifying. Without interruption by the slightest punishment. Or a whole sequence. Coercions. Verdicts. Confusions.

Willing inflictions. Above all. Each in relation to. Limitations. Lines.

                                                    (*A husha. A husha.*)

Diffused to avoid the entailed. (Of course.) No desire.

Nor the possibility of desire.

          The scandal vanquished.

                You will find nothing.

Luxuria

If you can't lay your hands on.   Lay my hands on.

Now.   Then.

                                                              Rain.

Ground wet.

If this is what it is like —   unhoused

quick pressed and released   up against.

                                                         A bit-lip moon.

Scent of —   taste of —

honey-suckled   fingers

damp   to your mouth.

Be afraid of and want not.

A wish-stone

swallowed whole.

Perhaps and very likely

there'll be pain.

Under   a broken rib —

an ache   beaten deep into the midline.

Believe in. What can be believed.

Rain.

Grief.

Skin.

LOVERAINHEAVY
RAINHEAVYLOVE
HEAVYLOVERAIN

Notes and Acknowledgements

The Roud Folk Song Index was the catalyst for "A General Tale."

"Lax Tabulation" was written as an ekphrastic response to michèle provost's art installation, *ABSTrACTS / RéSuMÉS: An Exercise in Poetry,* at the Ottawa Art Gallery. Others who responded to her work were jwcurry, John Lavery, Pearl Pirie, Carmel Purkis, and Grant Wilkins. Our material was presented at Ottawa's artist-run centre, Saw Gallery, in early 2010, in cooperation with the AB Series. For this opportunity, and for the artwork represented on the cover, I give ongoing thanks to michèle.

"Testamonium," a portmanteau of testament and testimony, is an extension of that response through a bifocal lens of Michel Foucault's *Discipline and Punish: The Birth of the Prison* and Simone de Beauvoir's *The Second Sex.*

A gift from Amanda Earl, Oliver Schröer's "Camino" incited "Luxuria".

Excerpts from earlier versions of *The Counting House* were published in *filling Station, Grain Magazine, 17 seconds,* and *The Peter F. Yacht Club.* I thank the editors of each.

Gratitude to the Canada Council for the Arts, the Ontario Arts Council, and the City of Ottawa for funding received and for continued support of the arts.

In addition to the people and organizational bodies above, my gratitude also to Silvija Barons, Steven Heighton, Jennifer Londry, John MacDonald, Marcus McCann, Christine McNair, Roland Prevost, Peter Richardson, Su Rogers, and Jennifer Still — for friendship and editorial eyes.

Thanks especially to Phil Hall.

SANDRA RIDLEY's first full-length collection of poetry, *Fallout*, won the 2010 Saskatchewan Book Award for Publishing, the Alfred G. Bailey Prize, and was a finalist for the Ottawa Book Award. Her second book, *Post-Apothecary*, was short-listed for the 2012 ReLit and Archibald Lampman Awards. Also in 2012, Ridley won the International Festival of Authors' Battle of the Bards and was featured in The University of Toronto's Influency Salon. Twice a finalist for the Robert Kroetsch Award for Innovative Poetry, Ridley is the author of two chapbooks, *Rest Cure* — and *Lift*, for which she was co-recipient of the bpNichol Chapbook Award.

Colophon

Manufactured as the first edition of *The Counting House* in the Autumn of 2013 by BookThug.

Distributed in Canada by the Literary Press Group: www.lpg.ca

Distributed in the United States by Small Press Distribution: www.spdbooks.org

Shop online at www.bookthug.ca

Type + design by Jay MillAr

Copy Edited by Ruth Zuchter